Frederick Douglass

Published in the United States of America by Cherry Lake Publishing
Ann Arbor, Michigan
www.cherrylakepublishing.com

Content Adviser: Ryan Emery Hughes, Doctoral Student, School of Education, University of Michigan
Reading Adviser: Marla Conn, ReadAbility, Inc.
Book Design: Jennifer Wahi
Illustrator: Jeff Bane

Photo Credits: © Matthew B. Brady/Library of Congress, 5; © G.H. Houghton/Library of Congress, 7; © The Life and Times of Frederick Douglass (1881)/ushistoryimages.com, 9; © Internet Archive Book Images/ Flickr, 11, 22; © North Wind Picture Archives/Alamy, 13; © Frederick Douglass and William Lloyd Garrison/Library of Congress, 15, 23; © Library of Congress, 19; © Everett Historical/Shutterstock Images, 21; Cover, 10, 14, 18, Jeff Bane; Various frames throughout, Shutterstock Images

Library of Congress Cataloging-in-Publication Data

Haldy, Emma E., author.
 Frederick Douglass / by Emma E. Haldy ; illustrated by Jeff Bane.
    pages cm. -- (My itty-bitty bio)
 Includes bibliographical references and index.
 ISBN 978-1-63470-479-3 (hardcover) -- ISBN 978-1-63470-539-4 (pdf) -- ISBN 978-1-63470-599-8 (pbk.) -- ISBN 978-1-63470-659-9 (ebook)
 1. Douglass, Frederick, 1818-1895--Juvenile literature. 2. Abolitionists--United States--Biography--Juvenile literature. 3. African American abolitionists--Biography--Juvenile literature. 4. Antislavery movements--United States--Juvenile literature. I. Bane, Jeff, 1957- illustrator. II. Title.
 E449.D75H35 2016
 973.8092--dc23
 [B]
                          2015026080

Printed in the United States of America
Corporate Graphics

table of contents

About the author: Emma E. Haldy is a former librarian and a proud Michigander. She lives with her husband, Joe, and an ever-growing collection of books.

About the illustrator: Jeff Bane and his two business partners own a studio along the American River in Folsom, California, home of the 1849 Gold Rush. When Jeff's not sketching or illustrating for clients, he's either swimming or kayaking in the river to relax.

my story

I was born in **the South**.

I came from a family of **slaves**.

My mother was taken from me.
I was just a baby.

My grandmother raised me.

I was sent to work in a house.
I secretly learned to read.

Why is it important to be able to read?

I ran away. I found safety in **the North**.

I got married. I started a family. I worked odd jobs.

I started telling people my story.
I told them why slavery was bad.

I became an antislavery leader.
I was famous and respected.

How would you tell people your story?

I wrote my story down.
I wanted everyone to read it.

I printed a newspaper. I asked people to join my cause.

Douglass, Frederick

NARRATIVE

OF THE

LIFE

OF

FREDERICK DOUGLASS,

AN

AMERICAN SLAVE.

WRITTEN BY HIMSELF.

BOSTON:
PUBLISHED AT THE ANTI-SLAVERY OFFICE,
No. 25 CORNHILL.

America went to war. The South fought the North.

The North won. The slaves were freed.

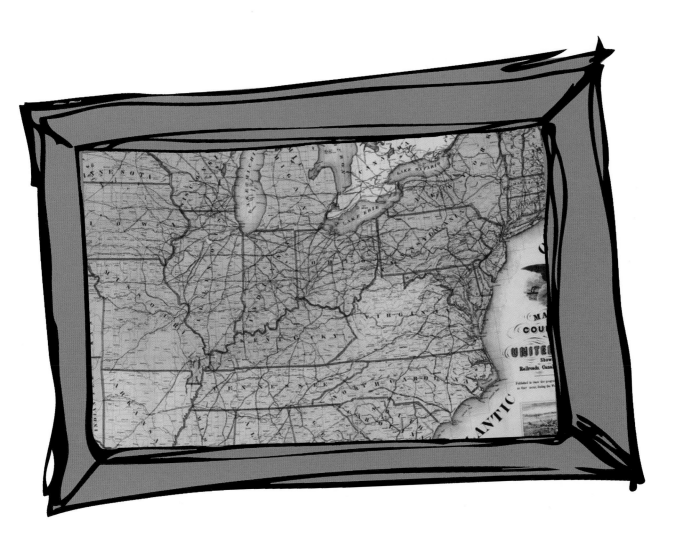

But my work was not done.
I wanted freed men and women
to get equal rights.

I kept writing. I kept speaking.

I fought for **equality** until the day of my death.

I was an accomplished man. I escaped slavery. I helped win freedom for my people.

What would you like to ask me?

1838

1800

Born
1818

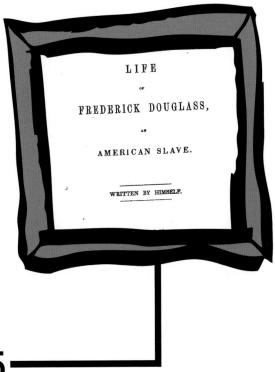

LIFE
OF
FREDERICK DOUGLASS,
AN
AMERICAN SLAVE.

WRITTEN BY HIMSELF.

1845

1900

Died
1895

glossary

equality (i-KWAH-li-tee) the right of everyone to be treated the same, without special advantages

slaves (SLAYVZ) people who are owned by other people

the North (THUH NORTH) the states in the northeastern U.S. that did not have slaves

the South (THUH SOUTH) the states in the southeastern U.S. that supported slavery

index

What Is the Theory of Evolution?

Robert Walker

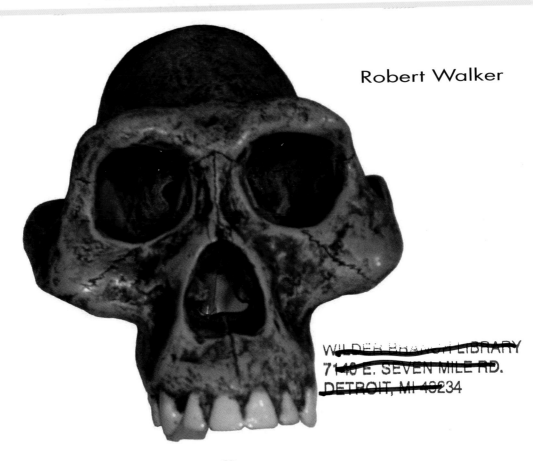

Crabtree Publishing Company

www.crabtreebooks.com

Author: Robert Walker
Publishing plan research and development:
  Sean Charlebois, Reagan Miller
  Crabtree Publishing Company
Editors: Jennie Worden, Adrianna Morganelli
Proofreaders: Kristine Lindsay, Molly Aloian
Project coordinator: Kathy Middleton
Editorial services: Clarity Content Services
Production coordinator and prepress technician:
  Katherine Berti
Print coordinator: Katherine Berti
Series consultant: Eric Walters
Cover design: Katherine Berti
Design: First Image
Photo research: Linda Tanaka

Photographs: cover lower right Fotolia, left and top right Shutterstock; title page Durova licensed under the Creative Commons Attribution-Share Alike 3.0 Unported license; p4 top Linda Bucklin/Dreamstime.com, lorboaz/Dreamstime.com; p5 Nancy Nehring/iStock; p6 Andy Lidstone/Shutterstock; p7 Jeremy Lessem/iStock; p8 Horia Bogdan/iStock; p9 United States Geological Survey; p10 mikeuk/iStock; p11 Richard Seefeld/licensed under the Creative Commons Attribution-Share Alike 3.0 Unported license; p12 Ghedoghedo licensed under the Creative Commons Attribution-Share Alike 3.0 Unported license; p13 Courtesy: National Science Foundation; p14 Stephen Martin/iStock; p15 top FunkMunk/CCL, The Jesse Earl Hyde Collection, Case Western Reserve University (CWRU) Department of Geological Sciences http://geology.cwru.edu/~huwig/; p16 A Bulldog Rat on a Plate from the work "A monograph of Christmas Island (Indian Ocean)" by Charles William Andrews (1866-1924) public domain/wiki; p17 Photograph by E.J. Keller, from the Smithsonian Institution archives/public domain/wiki; p18 top Public domain/wiki, lower left Public domain/wiki, right original in The Metropolitan Museum of Art/public domain/wiki; p19 Rachel Rosen; p21 top Nikolay Titov/iStock, Ralf Strohmeyer/iStock; p22 Project Gutenberg/public domain/wiki; p23 Public domain/wiki; p24

Reprinted in "Charles Darwin: His Life Told" in an Autobiographical Chapter, and in a Selected Series of His Published Letters, edited by Francis Darwin. London: John Murray, Albemarle Street. 1892. Julia Margaret Cameron/public domain/wiki; p25 Gary Hartz/Dreamstime.com; p26 Catalin Petolea/Shutterstock; p27 The Tree of life appeared in Darwin's "On the Origin of Species by Natural Selection" 1859/public domain/wiki; p28 left Didier Descouens licensed under the Creative Commons Attribution-Share Alike 3.0 Unported license, nugunslinger/CCL wiki; p29 Eric Isselée/Shutterstock; p30 Title page of the 1859 Murray edition of the "Origin of species" by Charles Darwin/public domain/wiki; p31 Print by Lock & Whitfield/public domain/wiki; p32 University of Zurich/Guérin Nicolas/licensed under the Creative Commons Attribution-Share Alike 3.0 Unported license; p33 top Public domain/wiki, Ruslan Dashinsky/iStock; p34 Madprime/Creative Commons Attribution-Share Alike 3.0 Unported license; p35 Andrew Buckin/Shutterstock; p36-37 Micah Weber/iStock; p37 top Published in "Follow the Money – The Politics of Embryonic Stem Cell Research" Russo E, PLoS Biology Vol. 3/7/2005, e234 http://dx.doi.org/10.1371/journal.pbio.0030234/CCL/ wiki; p38 kornilov007/Shutterstock; p39 Photo by M. Francisco/Bonemeal licensed under the Creative Commons Attribution-Share Alike 3.0 Unported license; p40 From "Voyage of the Beagle" by John Boyd/public domain/wiki; p41 Putneymark licensed under the Creative Commons Attribution-Share Alike 2.0 Generic license; p42 Willyam Bradberry/Shutterstock; p43 worldswildlifewonders/Shutterstock; p44 Ghedoghedo licensed under the Creative Commons Attribution-Share Alike 3.0 Unported license; p45 Nobu Tamura/www.palaeocritti.com licensed under the Creative Commons Attribution 3.0 Unported license; Reprinted in "Charles Darwin: His Life Told" in an Autobiographical Chapter, and in a Selected Series of His Published Letters, edited by Francis Darwin. London: John Murray, Albemarle Street. 1892/Julia Margaret Cameron/public domain/wiki; p46 risteski goce/iStock; p47 left Durova licensed under the Creative Commons Attribution-Share Alike 3.0 Unported license, 120/licensed under the Creative Commons Attribution-Share Alike 3.0 Unported license; p48 Qyd licensed under the Creative Commons Attribution-Share Alike 3.0 Unported license; p49 Mark Chen/iStock; p50-51 doga yusuf dokdok/iStock; p52 villiers/iStock; p53 Tim Vickers/public domain/wiki; p54 Pavel Tomanec/iStock; p55 Julie Fairman/iStock; p56 Jens L. Franzen, Philip D. Gingerich, Jörg Habersetzer1, Jørn H. Hurum, Wighart von Koenigswald, B. Holly Smith licensed under the Creative Commons Attribution-Share Alike 2.5 Generic license; p57 Catherine Yeulet/iStock.

Library and Archives Canada Cataloguing in Publication

Walker, Robert, 1980-
    What is the theory of evolution? / Robert Walker.

(Shaping modern science)
Includes index.
Issued also in an electronic format.
ISBN 978-0-7787-7198-2 (bound).--ISBN 978-0-7787-7205-7 (pbk.)

    1. Evolution--Juvenile literature.
I. Title. II. Series: Shaping modern science

QH367.1.W35 2011   576.8'2   C2011-900176-4

Library of Congress Cataloging-in-Publication Data

Walker, Robert, 1980-
    What is the theory of evolution? / Robert Walker.
        p. cm. -- (Shaping modern science)
    Includes index.
    ISBN 978-0-7787-7205-7 (pbk. : alk. paper) --
    ISBN 978-0-7787-7198-2 (reinforced library binding :
    alk. paper) -- ISBN 978-1-4271-9527-2 (electronic (pdf))
    1. Evolution (Biology)--Juvenile literature. I. Title. II. Series.

    QH367.1.W35 2011
    576.8--dc22
                                                    2010052628

Crabtree Publishing Company

www.crabtreebooks.com   1-800-387-7650

Printed in the U.S.A./022011/CJ20101228

Published in Canada
Crabtree Publishing
616 Welland Ave.
St. Catharines, ON
L2M 5V6

Published in the United States
Crabtree Publishing
PMB 59051
350 Fifth Avenue, 59th Floor
New York, New York 10118

Published in the United Kingdom
Crabtree Publishing
Maritime House
Basin Road North, Hove
BN41 1WR

Published in Australia
Crabtree Publishing
386 Mt. Alexander Rd.
Ascot Vale (Melbourne)
VIC 3032